THE SOUTHERN RAILWAY COLLECTION

Southern Railway Reflections
The London Area

Early morning at Clapham Junction, with Class N15 No 30795 *Sir Dinadan*
on the 7.30am Basingstoke to Waterloo semi-fast train on 29 March 1961.

The impressive sight of a Urie heavy freight tank engine, Class H16 No 30520, at Feltham Shed on 6 June 1957.

THE SOUTHERN RAILWAY COLLECTION

Southern Railway Reflections
The London Area

Terry Gough LRPS

· RAILWAY HERITAGE ·
from
The NOSTALGIA Collection

To Cynthia Ann who came from Lambeth

First published in 2005

British Library Cataloguing in Publication Data

A catalogue record for this book is available from the British Library.

ISBN 1 85794 235 3

Silver Link Publishing Ltd
The Trundle
Ringstead Road
Great Addington
Kettering
Northants NN14 4BW

Tel/Fax: 01536 330588
email: sales@nostalgiacollection.com
Website: www.nostalgiacollection.com

Printed and bound in Great Britain

All monochrome photographs are by the author

ABBREVIATIONS

BR	British Railways
GWR	Great Western Railway
LBSCR	London, Brighton & South Coast Railway
LCDR	London, Chatham & Dover Railway
LMSR	London, Midland & Scottish Railway
LNER	London & North Eastern Railway
LNWR	London & North Western Railway
LSWR	London & South Western Railway
SECR	South Eastern & Chatham Railway
SER	South Eastern Railway
WD	War Department

CONTENTS

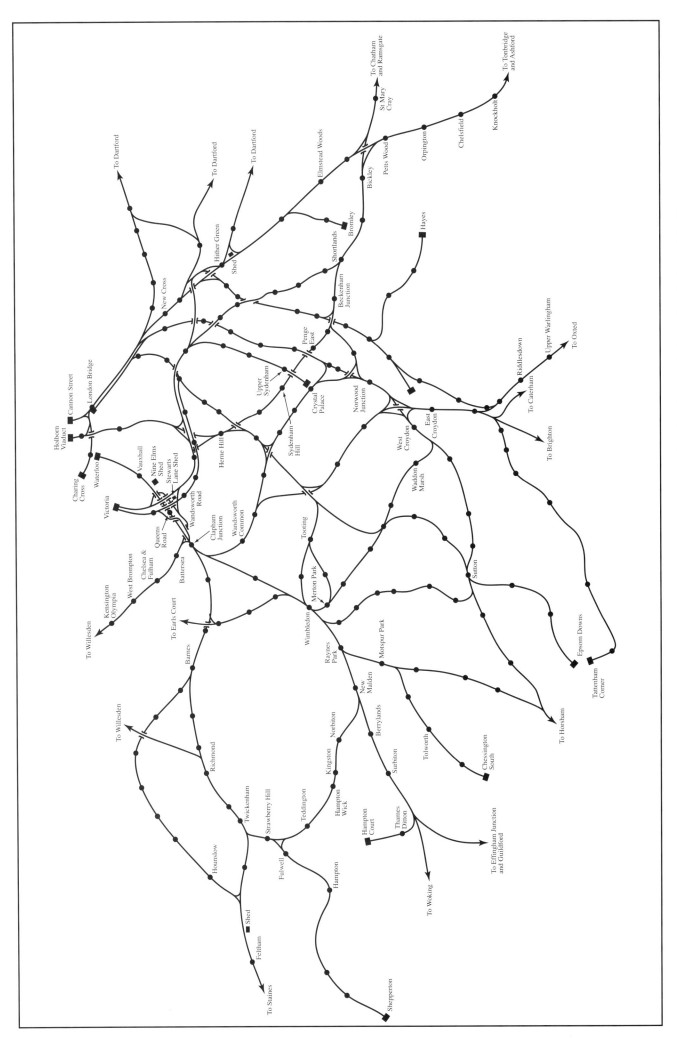

Simplified map of the former Southern Railway lines in the London area, showing the locations featured in the book and others of significance.

INTRODUCTION

The Southern Railway had by far the most complex suburban system of all the pre-Nationalisation railway companies. The system was a combination of the networks inherited from its three major constituent companies, the London & South Western Railway, the London, Brighton & South Coast Railway, and the South Eastern & Chatham Railway. In some cases these companies had developed lines in parallel, serving the same communities; the two lines running south to Crystal Palace from New Cross (LBSCR) and Nunhead (SECR) were a good example.

The LSWR and LBSCR had both introduced electric suburban trains. The LBSCR was the first, with an overhead pick-up system, opened in 1909 between Victoria and London Bridge, known as the South London Line. The overhead system was extended to Clapham Junction, Crystal Palace and the Norwood area within three years. Plans were made to extend to the other LBSCR suburban lines, but these were shelved during the First World War. Work was resumed in 1922 with electrification to Coulsdon (North) and to Sutton, both of which were completed in 1925 after the formation of the Southern Railway.

The LSWR decided to use ground-level pick-up and the first of the 'third rail' lines, from Waterloo to East Putney, was opened in 1915. The following year saw electric trains at Shepperton, Hounslow, Hampton Court and Claygate. The LSWR has its own generating station at Durnsford Road (Wimbledon), which was to continue in use well into British Railways days.

The SECR also planned to electrify its suburban network, but this never materialised and it was not until 1925 that the Southern Railway provided an electric service on the former SECR line from Victoria to Orpington via Kent House.

The SR thus inherited a suburban system operated by incompatible electric systems and by steam. It opted for third rail pick-up and the LBSCR system was abandoned by 1929. Expansion of the existing third rail system then began, so that by 1930 almost all suburban lines were electrified.

The SR also opened a number of new stations, including Birkbeck in 1930, Stoneleigh in 1932, Berrylands in 1933, and Falconwood in 1936. In the case of North Sheen and Whitton, it was coincident with electrification in 1930. The SR rebuilt several stations in the 1930s, including Kingston (1934), Surbiton (1937), Richmond (1937), and Twickenham (begun in 1938 and completed in 1954!). In addition, two major new lines were built. One was from Wimbledon to Sutton; with six intermediate stations, it was opened as far as South Merton in 1929 and throughout in 1930. The other line was planned to connect Motspur Park with Leatherhead via Chessington; opened as far as Tolworth in 1938, it was extended to Chessington South the following year. Construction from Chessington to Leatherhead was postponed following the outbreak of war and was never completed, the plans now having been formally abandoned. A few lines have closed, for example Tooting to Merton Park (1929), and Nunhead to Crystal Palace High Level (1954). Wimbledon to West Croydon and Woodside to Addiscombe both closed in 1997, but most of the trackbed has been used for a tramway, which opened in 2000.

For the new suburban electric services, the SR built, or in most cases rebuilt, a large quantity of rolling-stock. It inherited almost 500 coaches used in the pre-Grouping electric trains. It also had built under contract in 1925 some three-coach electric sets for the newly electrified lines on both the Western and Eastern Sections. From 1928 much of the old steam stock of all three pre-Grouping companies was converted into electric stock, which involved complete rebuilding with lengthened bodies. This policy of re-using old stock for new services continued throughout the SR period and was passed on to the Southern Region; new suburban sets of type 2-HAP were built in 1957 on underframes from 2-NOL sets built in 1934.

A new generation of suburban stock, the first of the 4-SUBs, was built at Eastleigh after the Second World War. The Standard all-steel 4-SUBs (with many variations) were built over the remaining years of the SR. Many of the pre-war sets were re-formed with the addition of a new or second-hand coach. The early BR suburban electric multiple units, such as the 4-EPBs, were very similar in style to the later 4-SUBs, and it was not until the introduction of the new suburban stock in the 1980s that a radical change in design was made.

Threading their way through the suburban network were the pre-Grouping companies' main lines. The former LSWR main line, through Clapham Junction, was opened from Nine Elms to Woking Common in 1838 and the terminus re-sited at Waterloo ten years later. The original motive power depot at Nine Elms was several times rebuilt and re-sited, until 1885 when its location remained until closure in 1967. An extension was added in 1910, which gave rise to two sheds in parallel, referred to as the old and new sheds. Nine Elms was one of the SR's most important sheds, providing motive power for many of the Western Section express trains from Waterloo to Portsmouth, Weymouth and the West of England, as well as more mundane local workings and the movement of empty carriage stock between Clapham Junction and Waterloo. The Portsmouth line was handed over to electric trains just before the Second World War, and diesels began to encroach on the other lines on an experimental basis at Nationalisation, although they posed no real threat until the mid-1960s. The end came with the use of diesel locomotives on all Exeter trains and the extension of electrification to Bournemouth in 1967.

The LBSCR opened the first part of its London to Brighton line from London Bridge as far as Croydon in 1839. It was not until later that the present-day Brighton main line from Victoria to East Croydon through Clapham Junction was built, after an unsuccessful plan to have a joint terminus with the LSWR at Waterloo. Victoria was opened in 1860.

The London, Chatham & Dover Railway also had its terminus at Victoria, and this was opened in 1862. Victoria continued to be the starting point for Central and Eastern Section trains throughout the SR period and to the present time. The LCDR main line ran parallel to the LBSCR line over the River Thames at Grosvenor Bridge, then passed its Longhedge Works toward Shortlands. The locomotive depot at Longhedge was later renamed Stewarts Lane, and it was from here that motive power was provided for the steam services out of Victoria.

The South Eastern Railway had its London terminus at London Bridge, with running powers over the LBSCR line through Norwood Junction to Redhill and thence eastward to Tonbridge and Ashford. London Bridge became a through station in 1864 with the opening of Charing Cross. The present main line through Chislehurst to Orpington and Tonbridge was not opened until 1868. This was electrified as far as Sevenoaks in 1935, but steam was of course still used on the main-line trains to Kent starting from Charing Cross. It was not until 1961 that the rest of the main line from Sevenoaks to Dover was electrified. Diesel multiple units were introduced on the Charing Cross to Hastings line in 1957 and electric units in 1986.

At Clapham Junction the Western and Central Section main lines briefly meet. From the London end of Clapham Junction one can observe simultaneously trains to places such as Reading, Alton, Bournemouth and Hampton Court. On the Central Section, trains to East Croydon, Redhill, Brighton and other South Coast towns, and the suburban services to places such as Epsom Downs and Sutton, all pass through Clapham Junction. Although most Central Section services were operated by electric trains, steam was regularly seen on the Oxted line up to the 1960s. Diesel multiple units took over in 1962 and from October 1987 electric units were used on almost all trains as electrification was extended to East Grinstead. In the intervening years all the other lines beyond Oxted had been closed, except to Uckfield, which is still operated by diesel multiple units.

In 1863 a line was opened from Clapham Junction to Kensington Addison Road, renamed Kensington Olympia in 1945. This had a steam service that survived into BR days, although it was very infrequent. It was shown in the main timetables of the 1950s, but not in the 1960s, despite the fact that it was still running. There were two morning and three evening trains advertised in such a way that there only appeared to be a service *to* Kensington in the morning and *from* Kensington in the evening. In fact, the same train did round-trip workings. The timings also varied with the day of the week and did not run at all on Sundays. After the demise of steam on this line, the trains were made up of a variety of stock, from old 4-COR electric or 4-TC units hauled by a diesel locomotive to both Western and Southern Region diesel multiple units. In the 1980s the service was reduced to two trains each way, again advertised as only in one direction. Kensington Olympia station is adjacent to the exhibition halls of the same name and in 1984 the Southern Region increased the frequency of the service to eight trains to Kensington and seven from Kensington each weekday. Unfortunately, this was not followed up with satisfactory publicity; the only reference made to the service, other than in the main timetable, was at Waterloo. It was of most value to passengers from the South and West, who, in ignorance of the service, would take the traditional route to Olympia on the District Line of the London Underground. From 1986 inter-regional trains were routed through Kensington, giving ten trains each way and, for the first time in years, a Saturday and Sunday service. A frequent passenger service from Clapham Junction to Willesden was introduced in 1994 and is currently operated by electric units. There is also a regular Brighton-Watford Junction service.

Another short but significant line is the SR's only underground line. Its official title is the Waterloo & City line, but it is often referred to as 'The Drain' and was opened by the LSWR in 1898. It was electrically operated from the outset, with a centre conductor rail. It was modernised by the Southern Railway, including the provision of new rolling-stock, which entered service in 1940; this has since been replaced by more modern stock The SR also converted the pick-up to its conventional third rail outside the running rails. The service was provided specifically for commuters and continues in this function today. Its service is very frequent, but restricted to Mondays to Fridays and Saturday mornings. London Underground took over its operation in 1994.

This book is a record of the Southern Region in the London area in the 1950s and 1960s, when there were still a few early Southern Railway electric units in use and steam was still common on the main lines. Within a few years of recording these aspects of railway operation, the scene totally changed and the lines are now operated exclusively with post-Nationalisation motive power and rolling-stock.

Terry Gough
Sherborne, 2005

WATERLOO TO CLAPHAM JUNCTION

Above A brisk start for 'King Arthur' Class No 30451 *Sir Lamorak* on the 2.54pm to Basingstoke, leaving Waterloo on 11 April 1962.

Below A reminder of days when Class T9 4-4-0s regularly worked into Waterloo, with No 30729 at the buffer stops after working a special train from Salisbury on 18 September 1960.

Above left An elevated view of the terminus in 1967. Just leaving is 'Merchant Navy' Class No 35008 *Orient Line* on a Bournemouth train. In the platforms are Class 33 and 'Warship' diesel locomotives, several Class 4-COR electric units and, in the suburban platforms on the right, two Class 4-SUB units.

Left The former LSWR M7s were used extensively on empty carriage stock workings to and from Clapham Yard. Nos 30052 and 30320 perform shunting duties at Waterloo on 25 March 1962.

Above A number of former GWR pannier tank engines were transferred to the Southern Region in 1959 to replace the ageing M7s. Class 5700 No 4621 pulls Bulleid set No 63 out of Waterloo on 30 July 1960.

Below More modern locomotives were also used for bringing in empty stock. In the last months of steam, Class 4MT No 80089 approaches Waterloo with a 12-coach train consisting mostly of Bulleid main-line stock. The arches under the station were used for a variety of activities, from wine storage to car repairs.

At the head of a special train at the beginning of its tour of suburban lines, ending later in the day at Guildford, is Class 0415 No 30582 of Lyme Regis fame and allocated, with its two sister engines, to Exmouth Junction Shed. On the left is Class 4-SUB electric unit No 4740. These units, the last to be built by the Southern Railway, attracted almost as much attention in later years as did the Adams engines on this occasion, 19 March 1961.

Above The mainstay of the semi-fast services to destinations such as Alton and Portsmouth & Southsea were the 2-BIL electric units. The similar but far less comfortable 2-HALs, built in the 1930s, were also used, and No 2650 has just arrived at Waterloo one morning in the summer of 1967.

Right An extraordinary sight on the down line through Vauxhall was this special train bound for Hampton Court and double-headed by Class 0298 Nos 30585 and 30587, which, with the only other member of the class, were normally based in North Cornwall. They were all allocated to Wadebridge Shed for use on the china clay trains from Wenfordbridge, which were hauled at a somewhat gentler pace than on this occasion, 2 December 1962.

Empty carriage workings between Waterloo to Clapham Yard: Class M7 No 30320 is in charge on 30 July 1960, while (*below*) sister M7 No 30052 is seen at Queen's Road Battersea.

Top Class 700 No 30701 enters Nine Elms Yard with a freight train on 3 August 1960.

Above Class H16 No 30519, with a train of Conflats, passes through Queen's Road Battersea on its way from Nine Elms to Feltham on 9 September 1959.

Right Class T9s were a rarity in London even nearly 50 years ago. No 30718 is seen on a local freight train, also near Queen's Road Battersea, on 24 September 1958. This was a rather degrading task for a locomotive that had been regarded as a most capable express passenger engine. Prior to electrification, T9s were regularly used on the steeply graded LSWR main line to Portsmouth Harbour.

Above Queen's Road Battersea, now called Queenstown Road, had platforms serving only the Windsor-side lines out of Waterloo. In early 1967 a train bound for Bournemouth passes the station hauled by a nameless 'Battle of Britain' Class No 34087 (formerly *145 Squadron*). The bridge in the background carries the South London line from Victoria.

Below An empty carriage stock working, with Class M7 No 30249 hauling a set of Bulleid coaches, is on its way to berthing at Clapham Yard on 3 August 1960.

Above Larger engines were also used to work empty stock back to Clapham Yard, after working their passenger trains into Waterloo. This is 'King Arthur' Class No 30777 *Sir Lamiel* hauling an odd collection of stock including an ex-GWR 'Siphon G' van, BR Mark 1 and Maunsell coaches, several Bulleid coaches and a Hastings line Pullman coach. This train is approaching Clapham Junction on 6 August 1961.

Below Clapham Junction always seemed to be busy and this is captured on 7 February 1962, with 'Schools' Class No 30926 *Repton*, a Class 08 diesel shunting in the yard, and Class H16 No 30520 arriving with empty stock from Waterloo.

Left Moving an empty train of Bulleid coaches into the yard on 3 August 1960 is Class M7 No 30035.

Below left A murky day in December 1960 sees Class W No 31918 dragging a heavy train through the down Windsor side of Clapham Junction, bound for Feltham but showing a Waterloo to Clapham Junction empty train headcode.

Above Class 5700 No 9770 enters Clapham Junction with a 12-coach train of empties from Waterloo on 21 September 1960.

Below A Suburban train from the Kingston Loop, worked by 4-SUB No 4730, passes Class H No 31542 running light on 10 July 1962.

Above Mixed traffic Class S15 No 30502 brings a handful of wagons from Reading along the up Windsor line at Clapham Junction on 22 December 1960. The station still gives the impression of being in the 1930s, with the original canopies and old-fashioned electric lighting, nameboards and panelled fencing. The lines to the right of the train are not electrified and the platform on the far right was used by the shuttle train to Kensington Olympia.

Left An unusual visitor to the Windsor side of Clapham Junction on 24 February 1957 was Class H2 No 32424 *Beachy Head*. This was working one of those complicated railtours that seemed designed to tax the ingenuity of BR for the benefit of railway enthusiasts!

CLAPHAM JUNCTION TO SURBITON

Above The down 'Bournemouth Belle' with 'Merchant Navy' Class No 35018 *British India Line* wends its Pullman coaches round the curve at Clapham Junction on 7 October 1961. This train was diesel-hauled after the end of steam, until it was withdrawn on 30 April 1972.

Right A 4-SUB electric unit, No 4103, is seen on the down main line between Clapham Junction and Earlsfield on 7 October 1961. This is a Waterloo to Guildford train, which ran non-stop to Wimbledon, then Surbiton and all stations via the New Line through Effingham Junction. Trains on this service did not call at Wimbledon in the rush-hour periods. This is one of a batch of ten sets built in 1942 and referred to as 'Queen of Sheba' trains; they were built to a similar style as the 2-HALs and accommodation was very cramped. One of the trailers had six First Class compartments, but these were never used as such, as First Class

was eliminated on all suburban trains before the units were brought into service. The total seating capacity for the whole unit was 468, about 80 more than in standard Bulleid 4-SUBs.

Left A semi-fast train to Bournemouth, the 10.54am from Waterloo consisting of an LNER Full Brake, a three-coach Bulleid set, a loose coach and an SR van, hauled by 'Lord Nelson' Class No 30857 *Lord Howe*, is on the down main line between Earlsfield and Wimbledon. In the background is Durnsford Road power station, and to the left the electric unit depot with suburban stock outside.

Below left Two de-icing units stand outside Durnsford Road power station on 19 March 1961. The leading unit is No 97, converted from the motor coaches of a withdrawn 4-SUB in 1959. This and similar units were later replaced by new de-icers derived from more modern 4-SUB coaches.

Above An up empty carriage working passes Durnsford Road Electric Depot behind GWR pannier tank Class 5700 No 4681 on 30 March 1961. On the right is the Railway Staff Halt for the electric depot.

Below The flyover takes the up local line over the down main line, so that from here the up and down local lines are adjacent. On the same day as the previous picture, 4-SUB No 4346 comes off the flyover forming an up Chessington South train. Emerging from the depot sidings is a Bulleid 4-SUB. The coaches on the far right are in 4-COR units, used mainly on the Portsmouth line.

Above A typical suburban scene at Wimbledon on 25 October 1961, with 4-SUB No 4348. Built as a three-coach unit in 1925, a Bulleid trailer was added in 1945, then a second Bulleid coach was added later to replace one of the original vehicles. It is working an up Guildford service via the New Line.

Below At Wimbledon one Sunday morning in May 1960, an engineers' train is hauled by Class 700 No 30701. The leading brake-van is of LBSCR origin and the one at the rear is to an SECR design, but built by the SR.

Right In Wimbledon Yard on 20 August 1965 Class U No 31619 of Guildford Shed is engaged in shunting duties. On the right the brake-van is BR-built and the coach, in engineers' use, is an ex-LSWR corridor Brake Third.

Below right Another view of the 'Bournemouth Belle', this time at Raynes Park headed by 'Merchant Navy' Class No 35028 *Clan Line*. On this occasion in May 1960 it is crossing from the down to the up main line as a result of engineering works. Now preserved, *Clan Line* can still be seen passing through Raynes Park on the 'Cathedrals Express'.

A down Portsmouth Harbour fast train passes through New Malden on the up fast line, a result of engineering works on the other side on 29 May 1960. The leading set is 4-COR No 3156 and the rest of the train consists of a 4-BUF and another 4-COR set.

The 11.30am Waterloo to Bournemouth train passes through New Malden on 8 May 1960 behind Class 5MT No 73118. A 'Mogul' on a breakdown train is on the up main line.

Left Bridge replacement work is taking place at the west end of New Malden over the weekend of 29 May 1960. A train of 'Walrus' wagons is being propelled on to the completed trackwork to offload its ballast.

Below left Deep in winter on the first day of 1962 is Class 4MT No 75076 thundering along the main line near Berrylands on a train from Basingstoke.

Above An M7, in this case No 30246, is a rare sight on the up through line at Berrylands on 16 September 1961. This is an empty carriage working from Oatlands Park to Waterloo, and the stock will later form an express train to Weymouth.

Right Another winter view shows an unidentified Class S15 in the cutting just east of Surbiton in January 1962.

NINE ELMS RUNNING SHED

Two of Urie's massive Class H15 4-6-0s, Nos 30486 and 30489, pose outside Nine Elms Shed on 8 March 1958. There were ten of these engines, built for mixed traffic work in 1914. No 30486 was withdrawn in 1959 and the other engine two years later.

The coaling plant at Nine Elms, seen here in the background, was built immediately after the formation of the Southern Railway. On 1 November 1961 Class E4 tank engine No 32473 (on the left) was one of several of this class used for shunting duties at Clapham Yard to augment the more numerous M7s and later the pannier tanks from the Western Region. Class S15 No 30505 and its sisters were frequently used on the semi-fast trains to Basingstoke and express freight train duties.

Above Class L1 No 31789 is out of use in Nine Elms Shed on 21 September 1960, carrying the 'Devon Belle' headboard. The engine was later stored at Eastleigh, where it was scrapped at the end of 1961. The 'Devon Belle' itself was short-lived, being introduced in 1947 and running only until 1954. Nine Elms Shed closed in 1967 and the site is now occupied by New Covent Garden Market.

Below The L Class 4-4-0s of the SECR were allocated to Nine Elms towards the end of their life. This photograph shows No 31768 on 21 September 1960; it was cut up the following year.

These views of Nine Elms Old Shed were taken on 6 August and 1 October 1961. Note that virtually every locomotive is facing inward, and the variety of classes from M7s and pannier tanks to Bulleid 'Pacifics'.

CLAPHAM YARD

Class E4 No 32500 shunts in the yard on 20 May 1960. This engine had been allocated to Nine Elms since Nationalisation and was dragged off to Ashford in 1961, to be cut up the following year.

A Bulleid 'Light Pacific' hides behind 'King Arthur' Class No 30765 *Sir Gareth* at Clapham Yard on 17 August 1962.

Former GWR pannier tank Class 5700 No 4681, formerly of Duffryn Yard Shed in South Wales and now allocated to Nine Elms, is shunting inspection saloon No DS 291 on 27 March 1961. This 12-wheeled vehicle was built by the LBSCR at Lancing in 1913 as the Directors' saloon. It was taken into Departmental use by the SR and corridor connections were fitted in 1933. It was withdrawn in 1964 and is now preserved on the Bluebell Railway.

Lightweight freight for a heavyweight locomotive: Class S15 No 30837 is seen at Clapham Yard on 7 February 1962. The rear vehicle is one of the bogie brake-vans built by the SR for express freight work.

Above Waterloo & City Line coach No S61 has come up for fresh air on 28 November 1965. It is at Clapham Junction sandwiched between match trucks in preparation for its journey to Eastleigh for overhaul.

Below One of the SR 'King Arthur' Class, No 30782 *Sir Brian*, built for the Eastern Section in 1925, has just arrived at Clapham Junction on a vans train from Eastleigh on 10 July 1962.

CLAPHAM JUNCTION TO KENSINGTON OLYMPIA

Above Class 2MT No 41292 stands in Platform 1 at Clapham Junction on 3 August 1960 waiting to take the 4.15pm train to Kensington Olympia.

Below Class Q1 No 33018 approaches Clapham Junction on a freight train from Hither Green to Feltham in December 1961. This is not strictly on the Kensington line, but it joins this line at Ludgate Junction after passing under the main line north of Clapham Junction.

Above left Class E1 No 31067 leaves Clapham Junction on a freight train for Willesden on 22 December 1960.

Left Class W No 31921 passes through Platform 17 of Clapham Junction with a Central Section freight train.

Above Class H No 31305 is coupled to the assortment of coaches that forms the Clapham Junction to Kensington shuttle service on 13 July 1962. It is arriving at Platform 17 on the last of the afternoon workings.

Below Three days earlier another H Class, No 31542, berths the same stock in Falcon Lane sidings near Clapham Junction, ready for the next day's service.

Above left Class M7 locomotives were rarely used on the Kensington service, but on 13 May 1959 No 30321 headed the 5.36pm from Kensington. It is seen here climbing towards Clapham Junction after passing under the main line. The train is a mixture of non-corridor pre-Grouping and SR-built coaches and a Maunsell Corridor Brake vehicle.

Left On 28 June 1962 the Kensington train is approaching Platform 1 at Clapham Junction behind Class H No 31542.

Above The stock for this service changed frequently, and on 17 August 1962 Class H No 31542 is hauling a Maunsell Open Third coach, a Corridor Brake and two BR non-corridor coaches between Clapham Junction and Battersea station, closed in 1940.

Below A milk train nears the site of Battersea station bound for Kensington, most unusually worked by Class O1 No 31370 on 13 May 1959.

Above Class 4MT No 42350 approaches the site of Chelsea & Fulham station with a freight train on 22 March 1961.

Below Class 2MT No 41292 passes the site of Chelsea & Fulham station with a rake of LSWR non-corridor coaches forming the 5.36pm Kensington Olympia to Clapham Junction train on 11 August 1958.

Above Class 5700 No 9659 passes Chelsea & Fulham signal box with a freight on 22 March 1961.

Below Class H No 31542 is seen again, this time passing the site of West Brompton station on 6 July 1962. This and the other intermediate stations were closed in 1940, but West Brompton re-opened in 1999. The station of the same name on the right behind the fence and shrubs is on the District Line to Wimbledon.

Above A van and milk train from Clapham Junction nears Kensington Olympia behind Class 2MT No 84022 on 22 March 1961. Earlier in the day this engine had worked a passenger train in the opposite direction. The Underground train on the right is the District Line shuttle service between Earls Court and Olympia.

Below Empty milk tanks from the SR, hauled by Class C No 31575, are waiting to enter Kensington Olympia on 9 February 1961.

Above A freight train from the SR, hauled by ex-LMSR 'Crab' Class 5MT No 42776, enters Olympia on 6 October 1961.

Below Class W No 31919, on a freight train from Willesden bound for East Croydon, passes through Olympia on the same day. There were 15 of these engines and they bore a strong resemblance to the SR 'Moguls'. They were built for inter-regional and transfer freights and were all allocated to London area sheds, notably Hither Green and Norwood Junction.

Above A smaller locomotive, GWR-designed Class 5700 No 9659, but a heavier freight train, struggles through Olympia on 23 March 1961. On the right is the District Line shuttle train to Earls Court, which ran only when the Exhibition Halls were open.

Below A special train to Robertsbridge and the former Kent & East Sussex Railway, headed by Class E1 No 31019, pauses at Kensington Olympia on 19 October 1958. Partly obscured by the steam is a large LNWR signal gantry. This train later stalled on the climb between Tulse Hill and West Norwood and had to be banked by a 4-SUB electric unit.

FELTHAM RUNNING SHED

Above Feltham Shed had an allocation of almost exclusively freight locomotives and was situated adjacent to the huge marshalling yard of the same name. The shed was modern in appearance, being constructed in precast concrete at the time of the Grouping to replace Strawberry Hill (see page 61). It had an allocation of between 60 and 90 engines, including large numbers of Classes S15 and Q1. Representatives of these classes are seen outside the shed on 31 July 1961.

Below Although most of Feltham's allocation was of former LSWR and SR engines, other railway companies would occasionally be represented. Photographed on 22 September 1960 are ex-SECR Class C No 31150 and ex-LBSCR Class E6 No 32408.

Above Feltham was famous for its allocation of the giant LSWR tank engines of Classes G16 and H16. The four members of the G16 Class, which were 4-8-0s, were built specifically for hump shunting, while the five H16s were 4-6-2s and were built for short-distance heavy freight work. In the foreground is Class G16 No 30493, and behind it Class H16 No 30520, outside the shed on 6 June 1957.

Below Two Urie engines, Class G16 No 30493 again, and Class S15 No 30505 at Feltham on 28 August 1956. The G16 and sister engine No 30492 were withdrawn in 1959, the two remaining engines of the class surviving until 1962. The S15 was also withdrawn in 1962.

Above left Shortly after the Second World War, Feltham had in its allocation 14 War Department 2-8-0 tender engines, designed by Stanier. These were to support the ageing and run-down pre-Grouping SR engines and were used mostly on inter-regional trains. Their stay was to last only a few years and by 1953 they had all been transferred away from the Southern Region. However, one of them, No 90261, returned briefly on 1 April 1960 after working a transfer freight from Hither Green. At that time the engine was allocated to Banbury on the Western Region.

Below left Another S15 locomotive, No 30498, stands alongside the shed on 22 September 1961.

Above Three locomotives are out of use at Feltham in the winter of 1962/63, representing three different generations of locomotive design. Nearest the camera is Class W 2-6-4T No 31923, designed by Maunsell for the SR in 1931. Behind is Drummond Class 700 No 30346, built in 1897, and last in the line is Class H16 No 30519. All three locomotives had been withdrawn a few weeks earlier.

Below The Feltham breakdown train stands outside the shed in 1967. The steam crane, No DS 80, was built by Ransomes Rapier, the bogie match truck was numbered DS 3087, and the mess and tool van, No DS 179, was converted from an ex-LSWR 'Ironclad' corridor Brake Third coach numbered 3187 in SR revenue-earning days.

Above Feltham normally only housed freight engines, but on 31 July 1961 'West Country' Class No 34003 *Plymouth* was on shed. The two Class Q1s flanking it are Nos 33018 and 33001.

Below An unusual vehicle, which was permanently stationed at Feltham, was an ambulance coach for use in the event of an accident in the yard. This was numbered DS 1119 and was formerly a LSWR wooden-bodied Brake Third coach, SR No 2975.

KINGSTON AND HOUNSLOW LOOPS

Right A Kingston Loop train, formed of 4-SUB unit No 4326 with a headcode signifying the clockwise route, waits to leave Raynes Park on 30 March 1961. The arrangement of platforms at Raynes Park was unusual in that they were staggered, a feature very common at former SECR stations, but not on the LSWR. This is the platform for the down local trains on the main line, while the Epsom line platform is to the right. There were no platforms for the up and down fast lines. The footbridge in the background connects these platforms with the country end of the up platform, an island with the outer face for trains coming off the Epsom and Chessington lines and the inner face for local trains from Kingston and Hampton Court.

Below At Kingston in March 1958 the steam crane, behind Class 700 No 30692, is waiting to place a new bridge section across the main road at the Norbiton end of the station.

The lunch period was a good time to visit Kingston, as there was invariably some shunting. On 2 August 1962 this was in the hands of Class W No 31924, seen pushing a few wagons into the huge goods shed.

The Kingston goods train was more commonly worked by a Class 700 or Q1, the latter being represented by No 33011 on 4 June 1962. In the background is Kingston Power Station and the cranes that were used for transferring coal from Thames barges.

Below First Class accommodation is available at no extra charge on this Kingston Loop train at Hampton Wick on 24 September 1958. This is the 12.50pm service from Waterloo via Richmond, and is most unusually being worked by 2-BIL No 2083 and 2-HAL No 2611, substituting for a failed 4-SUB. It was not until 1987 that the Kingston line had an advertised First Class service, and this was restricted to the first train of the day (Mondays to Fridays only), which left Waterloo for Shepperton at 4.00am.

Below A light fall of snow on 23 January 1958 gives a country look to Teddington, with Class 700 No 30339 entering the station on a freight train from Kingston.

Right A train of coal wagons is being shunted into Teddington Yard by Class Q1 No 33035 on 24 July 1963. Receding into the distance is a clockwise Kingston Loop passenger train.

Below right The daily freight train to Kingston, photographed between Strawberry Hill and Teddington, is being worked by Class 4MT No 80148 on 24 July 1963, recently transferred from Brighton to Feltham. It was later stored at Feltham until being sold for scrap in 1965. The electric depot, which used the buildings of the former steam shed that had closed in 1923, is behind the trees, and the old water tower can be seen behind the 4-SUB electric units.

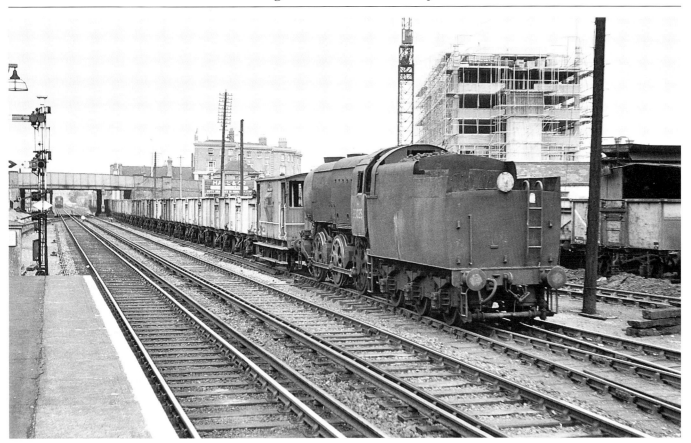

Above The Teddington to Feltham coal train ambles through Strawberry Hill behind Class Q1 No 33006 on 2 August 1963. Just beyond the station the Shepperton line forks right. Shepperton can also be reached from Teddington, thus forming a triangle, within which is the electric depot.

Left Withdrawn 4-SUB No 4324 awaiting disposal at Strawberry Hill on 25 March 1962.

Right De-icing set No 91 has been dumped out of use at the back of Strawberry Hill depot on 25 March 1962, where the locomotive coal stacks were once located. These two coaches, which were built in 1925, were taken from a withdrawn 4-SUB unit in 1960.

Below After electrification in 1916, Class M7 engines were rarely seen on the Shepperton branch. This photograph shows No 30053 on a special train from Waterloo near Fulwell on 5 July 1964. This engine was sold to a museum in the USA, but returned to England in 1987 and is now on the Swanage Railway.

Above left Seen in 1967, this typical small ex-LSWR signal box controlled the level crossing at Hampton on the Shepperton line. Most of these boxes have since been demolished, as traditional level crossing gates have been replaced by automatic barriers.

Below left The 2-NOL units were rebuilt from withdrawn steam stock in 1934-36 for use on the Central Section and the Windsor/Weybridge services, and were withdrawn very early in the Southern Region's stock modernisation programme. This photograph shows No 1860 at Twickenham on 12 August 1957.

Above The Christmas period always provided additional passenger and mail trains, often using older types of engines and rolling-stock. In the suburban electrified area 4-SUB electric units were used to convey parcels in the passenger compartments, to the complete exclusion of passengers. A parcels train is seen here passing through Twickenham on 27 December 1961, hauled by Class L1 No 31786.

Below Class S15 No 30839 shunts at Twickenham on 11 August 1965, and will later continue to Feltham. The far platform face is for down local services including anticlockwise Kingston Loop trains, while the two centre lines are for down and up Reading trains. The up local line is out of sight to the right.

Left A displaced 4-SUB unit! The Feltham crane is endeavouring to put No 4377 back on the rails at Hounslow on 21 December 1965. The unit was built in 1947 and was withdrawn after 30 years of trundling sedately round the Kingston and Hounslow Loops and other suburban lines.

Below Track-relaying is under way at Barnes on 7 April 1957. The Hounslow Loop, which is to the right, joins the line from Twickenham at this point.

HAMPTON COURT BRANCH

Above 4-SUB 'Sheba' unit No 4107, whose identity is almost masked by the snow, calls at Berrylands on a Hampton Court train on New Year's Day 1961. Berrylands was built in 1933 and has platforms only for local trains. It provided the basic facilities of a small booking office, waiting room and shelter on both sides, but even this was reduced when BR rebuilt the station.

Right The down Hampton Court branch was not usually worked by such exotic motive power. This is a special train from Wimbledon to Hampton Court, worked by Class 0298 Nos 30585 and 30587, back to back, leaving Surbiton on 16 December 1962. Both these engine still exist, one in the National Collection and the other in private ownership.

Left The Hampton Court line leaves the main line on a flyover built in 1915, 1½ miles west of Surbiton. This freight train, heading for Hampton Court behind an SR 'Mogul', is at Ditton Hill, between Surbiton and the junction, on 31 August 1961.

Below left The special shown on the previous page is seen here passing through Thames Ditton on its return journey on 16 December 1962.

Above The local freight train was commonly worked by a Class 700, but on 11 September 1961 Class U1 No 31905 was used, and is seen passing the modern signal box at Hampton Court. Just to the right of the engine is the old engine shed, in use by a private company.

Right The Hampton Court branch is only 1½ miles long, with one intermediate station at Thames Ditton. The terminus consists of an island platform with adjacent sidings for berthing stock. 4-SUB No 4308 has just arrived from Waterloo on 2 November 1961. This was originally a three-coach set of Class 1285 built in 1925 for the Western Section; the fourth coach, of similar style to a 'Sheba' trailer, was added in 1948, when the set was given its present number.

EPSOM AND CHESSINGTON LINES

Left At the down Epsom and Chessington platform at Raynes Park the driver of 4-SUB No 4337 waits for the doors to be closed before leaving for Horsham on 28 November 1961. This is one of the sets built in 1925 for the Eastern Section as Class 1496, with an all-steel trailer added in 1946.

Below Engineering works near Motspur Park during the first weekend of October 1955 resulted in a shuttle service between Tolworth and Chessington South. 4-SUB No 4648 crosses from the up to the down line at Tolworth before returning to Chessington South.

Right In the summer months, excursions were occasionally run from other Regions to Chessington South. This photograph, taken near Tolworth, shows a train of empty Gresley coaches worked by Class 5MT No 73081 heading for Chessington South in preparation for a return excursion to Biggleswade on 28 May 1960.

Below right Railway enthusiasts' specials rarely included the Chessington branch, but on 2 December 1962 Class H16 No 30517 was photographed near Tolworth.

Class Q1 No 33006 heads a train of empty coal wagons away from Chessington South on the return trip to Wimbledon Yard on 5 September 1964.

Bulleid 4-SUB No 4127, built in 1946, enters Chessington South at the end of its 14-mile journey from Waterloo on the same day. Class Q1 No 33006 has just run round the coal train seen on the previous page, which it has brought from Wimbledon Yard.

A DMU at Chessington South: this unit, consisting of vehicles E50029 and E50069, has been used for an excursion to Chessington South and is ready to leave on the return journey to Ipswich (not Penistone) on 21 June 1957.

WIMBLEDON TO WEST CROYDON

Above Members of the C2X Class were often seen in Wimbledon Yard, which was situated by the main line between the junctions for the West Croydon and Sutton lines. On 10 October 1961 No 32550 performs shunting duties.

Right During the day a trip was usually made to Merton Abbey, the only station on the line connecting Merton Park and Tooting. It was never electrified and closed to passengers in 1929. At Merton Park on 9 September 1959 the West Croydon passenger train passes Class C2X No 32447 on its way to Merton Abbey.

Left The only entrance to Merton Park station was on the Merton Abbey line side, seen on the left, although these platforms had been out of use since the Abbey line closed. The West Croydon trains used the platform out of view on the extreme right.

Below left A special passenger train was run to Merton Abbey on 20 April 1958, and is seen here reversing off the branch to continue its journey in the direction of West Croydon. The engine is Class H No 31521, with two pre-Grouping coaches forming set No 715.

Right Recently built Class 2-EPB No 5739 calls at Waddon Marsh Halt on 29 September 1957 with a Wimbledon to West Croydon service. Waddon Marsh Halt consisted of a single wooden island platform, and served nearby industrial estates.

Below Adjacent to the halt were sidings serving the gas works. On the same day Class E4X No 32477 is undertaking some shunting.

STEWARTS LANE RUNNING SHED

A freight train from the London Midland Region passes Stewarts Lane Shed in October 1958. The coaling plant was built in 1934 when the longhouse was rebuilt and the shed given its new name of Stewarts Lane. The bridge in the background carries the South London Line of the LBSCR from Victoria to London Bridge.

Class T9 No 30718 passes Stewarts Lane on its way to Nine Elms with a freight train on the same day.

Below Inside Stewarts Lane Shed on Christmas Eve 1960 is one of the former LBSCR Class E2 tank engines, No 32106. There were ten of these engines, most of which were allocated here. By the end of 1961 they had all been transferred to Southampton Docks, but were withdrawn within a couple of years. A new diesel and electric depot was built by the side of the engine shed as part of the Kent modernisation programme. The shed was closed to steam in 1963, was later used for the storage of surplus diesel locomotives and closed completely in 1999.

Below Stewarts Lane used Class P 0-6-0Ts for shunting duties in the nearby milk depot. No 31558 is seen there on 8 March 1958, where it had been allocated for at least the previous 13 years and where it remained until withdrawal in 1960. In the background is part of Longhedge Locomotive Works, built by the LCDR; this closed in 1912 when the Works relocated to Ashford.

Right Class L No 31776 of Brighton Shed stands at the side of Stewarts Lane Shed on 19 September 1957. Engines of this class were built in 1914 for the SECR and all 20 passed into BR ownership. Withdrawals began in 1956, this engine succumbing in 1961.

Below right 'Merchant Navy' Class No 35001 *Channel Packet* leaves Stewarts Lane in October 1958. On the bridge is a 4-SUB electric unit on an Orpington to Victoria service.

A few minutes after the photograph on the previous page *Channel Packet* pounds up the bank past Stewarts Lane Junction on its way to Clapham Junction with the Pullman stock for the 'Bournemouth Belle'. The rear of the train is passing under the former LSWR main line from Waterloo. The overbridge carries the LCDR (and later SECR) main line from Victoria to North Kent. On the right is Class Q1 No 33029.

Stewarts Lane Shed was responsible for providing the motive power for the 'Golden Arrow', which on 8 March 1958 was worked by 'Britannia' Class No 70004 *William Shakespeare*, one of two 'Britannias' allocated here in the 1950s.

LONDON TO CROYDON AND THE OXTED LINE

Above Several evening rush-hour trains for the Oxted line left from London Bridge's Low Level platforms, sandwiched between the SECR through lines to Charing Cross and the LBSCR terminus. On 23 February 1962 'West Country' Class No 34109 *Bideford* is working the 4.40pm to Brighton, while Standard Class 4MT No 80145 is on the 5.20pm to Tunbridge Wells West, both of which ran via Oxted.

Below Class 4MT No 80015 works the 4.20pm to East Grinstead at London Bridge on 23 February 1962.

Above A van train stands in the Low Level platform at London Bridge on 30 September 1961 behind 'Schools' Class 30917 *Ardingly*.

Right Steam at Victoria on 13 February 1962: Class 4MT No 75070 enters the station to collect some vans, while in the background is Class 4MT No 80142, which will shortly leave on an Oxted line train.

Class 4MT No 80142 stands at Victoria with the 10.08am train to Tunbridge Wells West via Oxted and East Grinstead on 13 February 1962.

A light engine, Class N No 31402, showing the Victoria to Brighton headcode, draws up for water at Victoria on 13 February 1962.

Left Class 4MT No 75070 enters Victoria with the 7.47am train from Tunbridge Wells West on 13 February 1962. This train took the longer route via East Grinstead and called at all stations, taking 2 hours to cover 44 miles.

Below left A portrait of Class 4MT No 75074 on Grosvenor Bank on 25 February 1962, showing a Brighton headcode in preparation for working the 9.38am from Victoria.

Right The 3.54pm Victoria to Brighton train passes Clapham Junction on 17 August 1962 behind Class 4MT No 75070. The first stop was East Croydon, then Oxted and Edenbridge Town, before reaching Eridge, where a portion was detached for Eastbourne. It then ran all stations (except Falmer) to Brighton.

Below Standard Class 4MT No 80140 works the 11.08am Victoria to Tunbridge Wells West train just south of Clapham Junction on 7 October 1961. The Western Section main line is on the extreme left. The 4-SUB electric unit on the right is on a Victoria to Epsom Downs service.

Above Motive power in the form of Class 4MT No 75069 was provided by Stewarts Lane on 28 May 1961 for the 9.38am Victoria to Brighton train. This train, which is seen near Wandsworth Common, ran via Oxted and Eridge and took twice the time to reach Brighton by this route compared with the main line.

Below One of the SR main-line electric locomotives, No 20003, is employed on a Newhaven boat train near Wandsworth Common on 6 August 1961. No 20003 was the first of these locomotives to be withdrawn, in 1968; the other two, of what was later Class 70, were withdrawn shortly afterwards.

Above Passing Wandsworth Common at speed on 13 February 1962 is Class 4MT No 75070 on a Victoria to Brighton via Oxted train.

Below In this view of Wandsworth Common looking towards East Croydon on 13 May 1962, Class 4MT No 80147 heads the 1.47pm service from Tunbridge Wells West to Victoria.

Left An up suburban train pauses at Norwood Junction on 22 March 1961. Set No 4305 was one of several sets built for the Western Section in 1925 as a 3-SUB (Class 1285), and, in common with all 3-SUBs, a fourth vehicle was added after the Second World War.

Below left An older 4-SUB, No 4540, is seen at Norwood Junction on 5 September 1955. The headcode 'V' indicates that the train is on a London Bridge to Selhurst via Forest Hill service.

Right A double-headed freight train at Norwood Junction is hauled by Class W No 31919 and Class E6X No 32411 on 5 September 1955.

Below The Class O1 0-6-0s of the SECR were very rarely seen in the London area; there were eight of them in BR times and they were allocated to Dover and Ashford. This example, No 31064, was allocated to Stewarts Lane for a brief period prior to withdrawal in 1958, and it is seen shunting at East Croydon on 19 September 1957. 6-PUL electric unit No 3015 is on the rear of a Victoria to Brighton train.

Above Class 4MT 42091 is about to enter Riddlesdown Tunnel with the 11.47am Tunbridge Wells West to Victoria train on 5 September 1959.

Below BR Standard Class 4MT No 80145 is working the 12.45pm train from Tunbridge Wells West to Victoria near Upper Warlingham on the same day.

There was plenty of variety of motive power on this line, and the train an hour later was hauled by Class U1 No 31898.

CRYSTAL PALACE BRANCH

Above Not all SR suburban lines prospered. The branch from Nunhead to Crystal Palace High Level closed in September 1954, and this is Upper Sydenham a year later.

Below Just before reaching the terminus the line entered a tunnel, seen here from the south end.

Above The imposing terminus at Crystal Palace High Level lay derelict for many months following closure.

Below Inside the station the poor state of platform 4 can be seen only six weeks after closure.

NORWOOD JUNCTION RUNNING SHED

Above In this line of stored locomotives outside Norwood Junction Shed on 19 September 1957, the two leading engines are both of Class E6, Nos 32413 and 32418. Behind them is the unique Bulleid diesel-mechanical locomotive No 11001, built in 1950 for shunting and transfer freight work. It spent the whole of its short life at Norwood Junction and was cut up at Ashford in 1959. Behind the diesel is another E6, No 32414. The shed was built by the SR to provide freight locomotives for the surrounding yards. Most of its allocation was of former LBSCR engines, but some SR-built Classes W and Q and diesel shunters were included. The shed was closed in 1964 and demolished two years later.

Left Class Q No 30533 stands outside the shed on the same day. This engine was transferred to Brighton in 1961 and the following year to Bournemouth, prior to being scrapped at Eastleigh in 1963.

Above right No 32411, seen here at Norwood Junction Shed on 5 September 1955, was one of only two E6s that had Class C3 boilers fitted in 1911, being re-classified E6X. This engine was withdrawn in 1959 and the other example in 1957.

Right Another unusual class was the E4X, which were E4s fitted with Class I2-type boilers. There were four of these engines, and No 32477 is seen on the right at Norwood Junction shed on the same day; it was withdrawn in 1959. The engine under the coaling stage is Class E3 No 32458.

VICTORIA TO ST MARY CRAY

Left This ramblers' excursion to Tenterden, taken as far as Robertsbridge by two Class Ls Nos 31760 and 31768, is almost ready to leave Victoria on 18 October 1959.

Below On 28 May 1961 a double-headed train bound for Kent and a 6-PUL electric train for Brighton are seen at Victoria. The two engines are Classes E1 No 31067 and D1 No 31739.

Right The empty stock for the 'Golden Arrow' enters Victoria behind Class 2MT No 84022 on 28 May 1961. This engine was built in 1957 and allocated to Ashford, then transferred to Exmouth Junction shortly after this photograph was taken. It only stayed there a few months and ended up at Crewe, where it was scrapped in 1964. In the foreground is 'Battle of Britain' Class No 34077 *603 Squadron*.

Below right No 34077 was at the head of a boat train from Victoria via Maidstone East. Many of the 'Battle of Britain' and 'West Country' Class locomotives were rebuilt by BR, resulting in a more conventional but still attractive outline.

Empty carriage stock for a Kent Coast train passes Stewarts Lane Junction on its way to Victoria in September 1958 behind Class D1 No 31145. A large carriage shed and storage sidings were situated adjacent to the old Longhedge Works and beyond Stewarts Lane Shed, which is just behind the camera. The 4-SUB in the background is on the Western Section main line from Waterloo.

An Eastern Section main-line departure from Victoria on 13 May 1959, with Class 5MT No 73041 on the 3.35pm to Ramsgate. Electric multiple units took over a month later.

Class N15 No 30782 *Sir Brian* climbs vigorously out of Victoria toward Grosvenor Bridge on 25 February 1962.

Above Electric Locomotive No E5005 leaves Victoria on 25 February 1962 with the 'Golden Arrow'. One member of this type of locomotive, later referred to as Class 71, is in the National Collection. The headcode '46' signifies a boat train from Victoria to Dover Marine via Herne Hill and Orpington. Various other headcodes were used for boat trains running between these two points, but taking different routes; for example, '13' ran via Catford and Maidstone East.

Below Another Kent express, the 10.35am to Ramsgate, is seen shortly after leaving Victoria, worked by Class 5MT No 73081. This was one of ten new engines of this class allocated to Stewarts Lane in 1955, working the trains to and from Kent until electrification in 1959.

Above 'Schools' Class No 30917 *Ardingly* is at the head of the 1.24pm Victoria to Ramsgate train in October 1958, on the elevated section of the main line between Grosvenor Bridge and Factory Junction. Built in 1865, it passed over the LSWR main line, in contrast to the original route, which went under it. The photograph was taken from the vicinity of Stewarts Lane, which was on the old LCDR route and was closed two years after the viaduct was built.

Below This up train is just beyond Factory Junction and is hauled by another 'Schools' Class, No 30913 *Christ's Hospital*, in October 1958. It had left Dover Priory at 10.15am.

Above 'Battle of Britain' Class No 34087 *145 Squadron*, on the 10.00am Victoria to Dover Marine train, has just passed Factory Junction where the two lines from Victoria (ex-LCDR and ex-LBSCR South London line) both meet the ex-LCDR line from the Clapham Junction direction. This photograph was taken from Wandsworth Road station on the South London line in September 1958; Factory Junction signal box is on the extreme left.

Below Class N No 31413 approaches Herne Hill with the 10.35am Victoria to Ramsgate train on 15 May 1959.

Left 'Merchant Navy' Class No 35001 *Channel Packet* works a down boat train near Sydenham Hill on 15 May 1959.

Below The 11.35am Victoria to Ramsgate train, with BR Mark 1 and Pullman coaches, is seen near Penge East on 15 May 1959. The engine is 'King Arthur' Class No 30806 *Sir Galleron*, the last of the class to be built. The Pullman coaches can be explained by the fact that, until the previous year, this train was known as the 'Kentish Belle'.

Right Class 5MT No 73081 runs through Beckenham Junction on the 12.35pm Victoria to Ramsgate train on 15 May 1959.

Below right An up coal train nears Shortlands in May 1959, hauled by Class N No 31408. There were 80 Ns built, and despite having one of the lowest numbers in the class, this engine was one of the last batch.

With Shortlands station in the background. Class 5MT No 73041 heads toward Dover in the spring of 1959 with an assortment of Maunsell and Bulleid coaches.

'West Country' Class No 34103 *Calstock* approaches Bickley with a Dover train on 15 May 1959. The colour light signals were brought into operation two weeks later. A train of the new electric stock for the Kent expresses is on the right.

Above Another train was photographed heading for the Kent Coast on the same day as the previous photograph. This is Class U1 No 31895 on an extra to Ramsgate near Bickley. Apart from the first member of the class, which was rebuilt from a K1, all U1s were new engines built at Eastleigh in 1931.

Below 'West Country' Class No 34026 *Yes Tor* takes a Ramsgate train to Victoria on 15 May 1959 and is seen near St Mary Cray.

HITHER GREEN RUNNING SHED

Right Hither Green Shed was built by the SR for freight locomotives, and its allocation included heavy freight engines such as Class W No 31925 seen here on 30 July 1960. Most of this class were withdrawn in 1963 and the class was extinct the following summer. It also had several diesel shunters and, after withdrawal of steam, several Type 3 diesels.

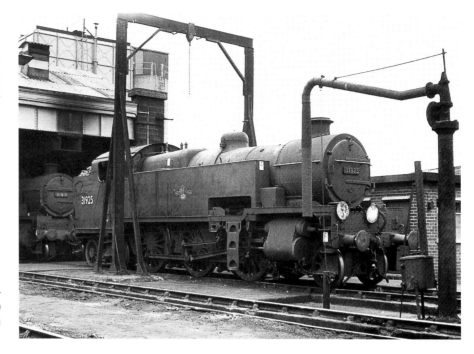

Below Hither Green also had some former SECR Class C engines, including Nos 31690 and 31686, both of which were withdrawn in 1962.

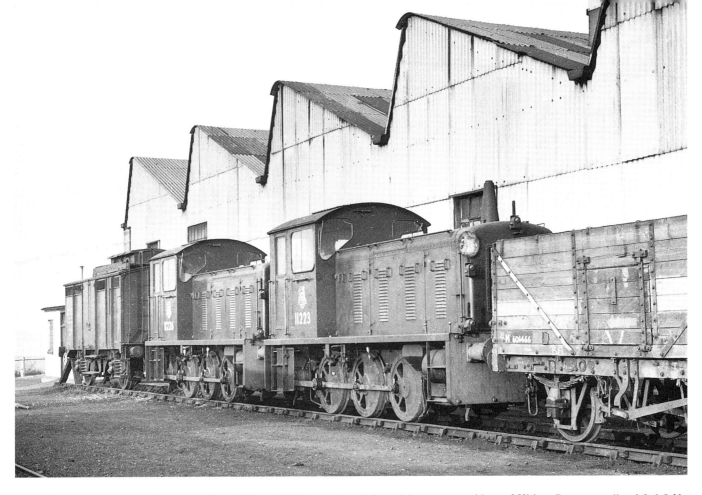

Above Two diesel-mechanical shunters, Nos 11223 and 11226, stand alongside the shed shortly after arrival in 1957. They later became known as Class 04 and were renumbered D2253 and D2256, being withdrawn in 1969 and 1967 respectively.

Below A long-term resident of Hither Green was diesel 0-6-0 No DS1173, which was used in the engineers' department adjacent to the running shed. It is seen on 6 December 1957 in the company of No 11221. DS1173 was built in 1947, later renumbered D2341 and withdrawn in 1968.

CHARING CROSS TO ORPINGTON

Above Two four-coach double-deck trains were built at Eastleigh in 1949 and used on the Dartford line for almost all of their lives. They were Classified 4-DD, and this is No 4001 at Charing Cross in 1967. Both units were withdrawn in 1971, and one still exists in private hands.

Below The other interesting and regular sight at Charing Cross was the diesel multiple units specially built for the Hastings line in 1957 to replace steam-hauled trains. This is No 1016 of Class 6L (later 202) at Charing Cross forming the 10.33am service to Hastings in the early 1980s.

Above and below 'Schools' Class No 30939 *Leatherhead* approaches Waterloo East on the 5.08pm Hastings to Charing Cross train on 3 June 1958, then, some 20 years later, Class 6L No 1016 is seen at the same location.

Left A Hastings-bound train formed of Unit No 1018 pauses at Waterloo East, while a 1951-designed electric unit of Class 4-EPB No 5437 heads for Charing Cross with a suburban service. Platforms at Waterloo East are lettered rather than numbered to avoid confusion with the Western Section terminus.

Below left BR electric and SECR steam side by side at London Bridge in the summer of 1961.

Right Unit No 1018 is seen again, this time passing through London Bridge. Most Hastings trains did not stop here.

Below It was worth the effort of an early start from home in Surbiton to see the 7.24am train from London Bridge to the Kent Coast in the last weeks of steam to Kent, as on several occasions it was worked by Class D1 No 31739. It took 3½ hours to reach Margate via Ashford and Dover. Early morning mist mingles with steam as the train waits to leave London Bridge on 5 June 1961.

The same train as on the previous page is seen leaving London Bridge a few days later (*above*), and passing through New Cross on the same day (*below*). This was made possible by the photographer travelling on an electric train that left London Bridge at the same time but arrived at New Cross a minute before the steam train.

An inter-regional freight train passes Hither Green Shed on 30 July 1960, hauled by former LNER Class J50 No 68989 of Hornsey Shed (*above*), and Class W No 31925 takes an up freight train past Hither Green on the same day.

During the last year before the elimination of steam into Kent and the final phase of electrification, many former steam workings were in the hands of diesel locomotives. This was the case at the end of July 1960 when new Class 3 diesel locomotive No D6517 worked the 10.35am Charing Cross to Deal train near Elmstead Woods (*above*). A few minutes later a down boat train for Dover Marine passed the same spot hauled by 'West Country' Class No 34003 *Plymouth*.

Above 'West Country' Class No 34005 *Barnstaple* heads the 11.10am train from Charing Cross to Ramsgate near Elmstead Woods on 30 July 1960.

Below 'West Country' Class No 34100 *Appledore* passes Orpington with the 4.32pm train from Charing Cross to Margate on 30 July 1960. There was an electric depot here, which can be seen in the right background.

Class 5MT No 73089 passes Chelsfield on 23 May 1958 with the 11.48am Charing Cross to Ashford service.

Above Approaching Knockholt on 23 May 1958 is the 12.20pm from Charing Cross to Hastings, as usual worked by a member of the 'Schools' Class, on this occasion No 30932 *Blundells*.

Below Class 5MT 73080 leaves the London area behind as it passes through the countryside near Knockholt, only 16 miles from Central London, on its way to Dover.

INDEX OF LOCATIONS